C000077287

THE SECRET OF
POWER FROM ON HIGH

THE SECRET OF
POWER FROM ON HIGH

Andrew Murray

CLC
PUBLICATIONS
Fort Washington, PA 19034

The Secret of Power from On High
Published by CLC Publications

U.S.A.
P.O. Box 1449, Fort Washington, PA 19034

UNITED KINGDOM
CLC International (UK)
Unit 5, Glendale Avenue, Sandycroft, Flintshire, CH5 2QP

© 1998 CLC Publications
All rights reserved
This printing 2017

Printed in the United States of America

ISBN (trade paper): 978-1-61958-268-2
ISBN (e-book): 978-1-61958-269-9

Unless otherwise noted, all Scripture quotations are from the Holy Bible, New King James Version, copyright © 1979, 1980, 1982 by Thomas Nelson, Inc. Used by permission. All rights reserved.

Scripture quotations marked KJV are from the Holy Bible, King James Version,1611.

Italics in Scripture quotations are the emphasis of the author.

Cover design by Mitch Bolton.

INTRODUCTION

SOME time ago I saw an advertisement for a little book, *Prayer Made Easy*. At first I thought that if prayer was made too easy, it would lose its power; but I was so anxious to help those who were weak in prayer that I ordered a copy of the book, and I found that the writer had discovered the secret that it is only as the *Holy Spirit* teaches us to pray that our prayer will have power and be a joy to us. I felt that here indeed was a deep truth. It reminded me that so many know nothing of what the Holy Spirit can do for them.

I found some simple, helpful thoughts in the book, and these suggestions I shall use in the first chapters of *The Secret of Power from On High*. I shall then go on and try to help God's children exercise the great and wonderful privilege of close fellowship with God in prayer through the Holy Spirit, and to explain something of what is meant by a life of all-prevailing intercession.

In earlier booklets I have dealt with the adoration of God the Father and of personal intercourse with Christ the Son, and I would now lead my readers to consider their relation to the Holy Spirit in regard to prayer, and help them to realize what an unspeakable privilege it will be to take time every day to call upon the Spirit and to surrender themselves entirely to His guidance. When the prayer meetings held at the time of Pentecost are over, many feel that they need help in studying God's Word at home and to be led into a realization of the silent but mighty work which God's Spirit will do in them. Christians should not remain "babes in Christ" (1 Cor. 3:1), but should grow up as spiritual men to know the Lord Christ and to serve Him, to be witnesses to those around them, and to be a blessing to all with whom they come into contact.

Without spiritual guidance, Christians often find difficulty in understanding and appropriating the teaching of St. Paul's epistles in regard to the work of the Spirit—teaching which is necessary "for the equipping of the saints" (Eph. 4:12), whereby the body of Christ is built up into a "perfect man, to the measure of the stature of the fullness of Christ" (4:13). This pocket companion seeks to give help and teaching to all seekers after the life which is wholly surrendered to the leading of the Holy Spirit. The great truths regarding the work of the Spirit are presented as simply as possible, that the reader may be led to see how important it is to be changed into His image from glory to glory as by the Spirit of the Lord.

I pray that our Heavenly Father may grant great and new thoughts of His wonderful love, and a full measure of the blessings He is waiting to bestow.

ANDREW MURRAY

The Dispensation of the Spirit

"How much more will your heavenly Father give the Holy Spirit to those who ask Him!"

Luke 11:13

THE writer of a little book on prayer tells us that he has learned through his own experience the secret of a better prayer life, and would gladly pass on that which has helped him. As he was meditating on prayer, the great thought came with power that we are now living in the dispensation of the Spirit. He says: "I felt deeply that in this time of the working of the Holy Spirit, all we may do in God's service is of little value unless it is inspired by the power of the Holy Spirit. This brought me to the well-known, precious, and inexhaustible text, 'How much more shall your Heavenly Father give the Holy Spirit to them that ask Him?' (KJV)."

I felt anew that the main thing for each of us is to receive, afresh from the Father, the Holy Spirit for our daily needs and daily life. Without this we cannot please God, nor can we be of any real help to our fellow men. This brought the further thought that our prayers, if they are to raise our lives to fulfill God's purpose, must have their origin in God Himself, the highest source of power. Water cannot rise higher than its source. And so it happens that if the Holy Spirit prays through us, as human channels or conduits, our prayers will rise again to God who is their source, and the prayers will be answered by the Divine working in ourselves and in others. "I believe more and more," says the writer, "that the Christian life of each one of us depends chiefly on the quality of our prayers and not on the quantity."

What material for thought is here—for deep meditation, for earnest prayer! When you pray today, ask the Heavenly Father to give you the Holy Spirit afresh for this day. He yearns to do it.

Father, grant me *now* the working of Your Holy Spirit, that I may learn to pray.

The Fruit of the Spirit

The fruit of the Spirit is love, joy, peace, longsuffering, kindness, goodness, faithfulness, gentleness, self-control.

Galatians 5:22–23

WE have seen what are the first two lessons on prayer: We must pray the Father every morning to give us the Spirit anew, and then we must pray the Spirit to teach us and help us. Here is a third lesson: commit to memory the text at the head of this chapter.

Christians often think that they have only to ask God to teach them to pray and He will do it at once. This is not necessarily the case. What the Spirit usually does is to strengthen our spiritual lives so that we then are able to pray better. Whenever we ask Him to teach us something, it is important that we open our hearts to His gracious influence so that our desires are stirred, and we first of all surrender ourselves to the working of the Spirit. This surrender consists in naming before Him the gifts of the Spirit, with an earnest prayer to be filled with these fruits. So the benefit of learning the text by heart will be that as we pray for the teaching of the Spirit we may say: "Here is my heart; fill it with the fruits of the Spirit."

Think of the first three fruits: *love, joy, peace*—the three chief characteristics of a strong faith life. *Love*—love to God and to Christ, to the brethren and to all men.

Joy—the proof of the perfect fulfillment of every need, including courage and faith for all the work we have to do. *Peace*—the blessed state of undisturbed rest and security in which the peace of God that passes all understanding can keep our hearts and minds (see Phil. 4:7).

In Christ's last discourse with His disciples He used these three words with the word "My" before them: "Abide in *My love*" (John 15:9). "That *My joy* may remain in you" (15:11). "*My peace* I give to you" (14:27). Shall we not lay before the Spirit, as the great desire of our hearts, a request that He make these fruits reach perfection within us? Then at last we shall be able to pray aright and feel free to ask more and more from our Heavenly Father.

Led by the Spirit

*As many as are led by the Spirit of God,
these are sons of God.*

Romans 8:14

LET us now consider four other fruits of the Spirit: *longsuffering, kindness, goodness, gentleness.* These four words all denote attributes of the Godhead. They will reach maturity in us through much prayer for the working of the Holy Spirit. Think of what they mean.

Longsuffering—In the Old Testament, in the time of Moses, God's longsuffering was praised. All Scripture bears witness to the wonderful patience with which God dealt with sinful man, until we come to the word in Second Peter 3:9: "The Lord . . . is longsuffering toward us, not willing that any should perish but that all should come to repentance." This attribute of God, the Spirit will make a characteristic of our lives so that we too may exercise a divine patience with all sin and wrong, so that souls may be saved.

Kindness—What wonderful things we read in the Psalms about God's goodness and *kindness*, which are from everlasting to everlasting. "As the heavens are high above the earth, so great is His mercy toward those who fear Him" (Ps.103:11). God works in our hearts this same goodness and mercy toward all the sin and wretchedness around us.

Goodness—"No one *is* good but One, *that is*, God" (Matt. 19:17). All goodness comes from Him, and He gives to His children according as each heart asks and desires. And this goodness is manifested in sympathy and love to all who are in need.

Gentleness—We read in Psalm 18:35: "Your gentleness has made me great." But it was chiefly in God's Son that the divine gentleness was shown. Jesus says: "Learn from Me, for I am gentle and lowly in heart" (Matt. 11:29). Paul entreats his readers "by the meekness and gentleness of Christ" (2 Cor. 10:1). The Holy Spirit, too, the gentle Dove, longs to impart the ripe fruit of gentleness to our hearts.

Is it not a wonderful thought that these four attributes of God, which are the characteristics of God's work among sinners, may be brought to ripeness in our hearts by the Holy Spirit, so that we in all our ways and conversation may be like the Gentle and Lowly One?

The Spirit of Faith

Since we have the same spirit of faith . . . we also believe.
Second Corinthians 4:13

DO you begin to realize why it is so important to commit to memory the text, Galatians 5:22–23? It will strengthen the desire in our hearts to have and to hold the fruits of the Spirit within us. Our expectation of the blessing God will give will be enlarged. Let us pause a while on the two last fruits of the Spirit —faithfulness and self-control.

When the disciples asked the Lord: "Why could we not cast [the evil spirit] out?" (Mark 9:28), His reply was: "This kind can come out by nothing but prayer and fasting" (9:29). Their faith was not powerful enough, and even if they had prayed they had not the zeal and self-sacrifice needed for prevailing prayer. Here we see the union of faithfulness and self-control.

Faithfulness is a fruit of the Spirit—and leads the seeking soul to depend on God alone. Faith believes God's Word, clings to Him, and waits in perfect trust that His power will work within us all that He has promised. The whole life of the Christian each day is a faith life.

Let us now think of self-control, or temperance. This refers in the first place to eating and drinking, and leads us to restraint, carefulness, and unselfishness in our conversation, our desires, in all our intercourse with one another. Our motto should be: "Forsaking all worldly desires, to live righteously and godly and temperately in all things" (see Titus 2:12). Temperate in all our dealings with the world and its temptations. Righteous in the doing of God's will. Devout in a close communion with God Himself.

Faithfulness and self-control are both fruits of the Spirit. When we ask the Spirit to teach us to pray, we open our hearts towards Him in order that He may grant us these fruits of the Spirit, faithfulness and self-control, to influence our daily lives in our intercourse with God and man.

Learn this text by heart, and let the promptings of the Spirit in your heart each day lead you to the Father, so that He may grant the fruits of the Spirit in your inner life, which will then be seen in all your actions.

Worship God in the Spirit

We are the circumcision, who worship God in the Spirit, rejoice in Christ Jesus, and have no confidence in the flesh.

Philippians 3:3

The remarks of the past four days serve as preparation for the matter of prayer itself. We have already come to the Father with a prayer for the Holy Spirit. We have invoked the guidance of the Holy Spirit. Now we begin to pray.

First, we pray to God the Father, thanking Him for all the blessings of this life. We acknowledge our entire dependence and impotence, and express our trust in His love and care for us. We wait before Him until we have the assurance that He sees and hears us. Then we direct our prayer to the Lord Jesus, and ask for grace to abide in Him always, for without Him we can do nothing. We look to Him as our Lord, our Preserver, our Life, and give ourselves into His keeping for the day. We give utterance to our faith in His infinite love and the reality of His presence with us.

Lastly, we pray to the Holy Spirit. We have already prayed to Him for guidance. We now ask Him to strengthen us in the faith, that what we have asked of the Father and the Son may be truly wrought in us. He is the Dispenser of the power and gifts of the Father and of the Lord Jesus; all the grace we need must be the result of the working of the Spirit within us. Our text says that we serve God in the Spirit, we glory in the Lord Jesus, and have no confidence in the flesh. We have no power to do the thing that is good. We count on the Lord Jesus, through the Holy Spirit, to work within us. Let us take time to think and meditate on these truths. It will help to strengthen our faith if we repeat the text of Galatians 5:22–23, asking God to grant these fruits in our lives. As we surrender ourselves wholly, we shall have boldness by faith to accept the working of the Holy Spirit in our hearts.

Intercession

Pray for one another.

James 5:16

THERE is much value in intercession, and it is an indispensable part of prayer. It strengthens our love and faith in what God can do and is a means of bringing blessing and salvation to others. Let us learn the lesson thoroughly: Prayer should not be for ourselves alone but chiefly for others. Let us begin by praying for those who are near and dear to us, those with whom we live, that we may be of help to them and not a hindrance. Pray for divine wisdom, for thoughtfulness for others, for kindliness, for self-sacrifice on their behalf.

Pray for all your friends, and all with whom you come into contact. Pray that you may watch in prayer for their souls. Pray for all Christians, especially for ministers and those in responsible positions.

Pray for those who do not yet know the Lord as their Savior. Make a list of the names of those whom God has laid upon your heart and pray for their conversion. You belong to Christ; He needs you to bring to Him in prayer the souls of those around you. The Holy Spirit will strengthen you to an active love in watching for souls. Pray, too, for all poor and neglected ones.

Pray for the heathen, and for all mission work. Use a mission calendar, with daily subjects of prayer, and bear on your heart before God the missionaries, evangelists, teachers, and new believers among the heathen.

Do you think this will take too much time? Just think what an inconceivable blessing it is to help souls through your prayers. So look to the Holy Spirit for further guidance. If this intercession takes too much time in your morning watch, then take some time later in the day. Cultivate the feeling: "I am saved to serve." You will taste the great joy of knowing that you are living even as Jesus Christ lived on earth—to make God's love known to others.

Time

What! Could you not watch with Me one hour?
Matthew 26:40

ONE who wishes to pray as we have indicated in our previous meditations might say: "I think I could do all that in ten minutes' time." Very well, if ten minutes is all the time that you can give, see what you can do in that time. Most people can spare more time. If they will only persevere from day to day, with their hearts set on prayer, time will come of its own accord.

Is it possible that Christians can say that they cannot afford to spend a quarter or half an hour alone with God and His Word? When a friend comes to see us, or we have to attend an important meeting, or there is anything which is to our advantage or pleasure, we find time easily enough.

And God, the great God, who has a right to us and who in His wondrous love longs for us to spend time with Him, that He may communicate to us His power and grace—can we find no time for fellowship with Him? Even God's own servants, who might consider it their special privilege to be much with Him in prayer to receive the fullness of power—even His servants are so occupied with their own work that they find little time for that which is all-important—waiting on God to receive power from on high.

Dear child of God, let us never say, "I have no time for God." Let the Holy Spirit teach us that the most important, the most blessed, the most profitable time of the whole day is the time we spend alone with God. Pray to the Lord Jesus, who in His earthly life experienced the need of prayer; pray to the Holy Spirit, who will impress upon us this divine truth. As indispensable to me as the bread I eat and the air I breathe is communion with God through His Word and prayer. Whatever else is left undone, God has the first and chief right to my time. Then only will my surrender to God's will be full and unreserved.

The Word of God

The word of God is living and powerful.
Hebrews 4:12

I find it a great help to use much of God's Word in my prayers. If the Holy Spirit impresses a certain text upon my mind, I take it to the throne of grace and plead the promise. This habit increases our faith, reminds us of God's promises, and brings us into harmony with God's will. We learn to pray according to God's will and understand that we can only expect an answer when our prayers are in accordance with that will (see 1 John 5:14).

Prayer is like fire. The fire can only burn brightly if it is supplied with good fuel. That fuel is God's Word, which must not only be studied carefully and prayerfully but must be taken into the heart and lived out in the life. The inspiration and powerful working of the Holy Spirit alone can do this.

By thoughts such as these we gain a deeper insight into the value and power of God's Word as a seed of eternal life. We are all familiar with the characteristics of a seed—a small grain in which the life-power of a whole tree slumbers. If it is placed in the soil it will grow and increase and become a large tree.

Each word or promise of God is a seed containing a divine life in it. If I carry it in my heart by faith, love it and meditate on it, it will slowly but surely spring up and bring forth the fruits of righteousness. Think over this until you gain the assurance: Although my heart seems cold and dead, the Word of God will work within me the disposition promised in His Word.

The Holy Spirit uses both the Word and prayer. Prayer is the expression of our human need and desire. The Word of God is the means that the Holy Spirit teaches us to use as a guide to what God will do for us. When these are united, the resulting flame becomes a demonstration of the secret working of the Holy Spirit in our hearts, by which God Himself fulfills His promise and gives us what we could not obtain without the help of the Spirit.

In the Name of Christ

Whatever you do in word or deed, do all in the name of the Lord Jesus, giving thanks to God the Father through Him.

Colossians 3:17

AT the close of your prayer it is always well to add a request for the "Spirit of Remembrance"—He who will "bring to your remembrance all things" (John 14:26) all through the day—so that the prayers of the morning may not be counteracted by the work of the day. Read the text at the head of this passage once more, prayerfully.

Have you ever realized that this is a command? Is it the aim of your life to obey it and to fulfill its injunctions? This may be difficult, but it is not impossible or God would not have asked it of us. God's Word has a wonderful power to preserve the spirit of thanksgiving in our lives. When we rise in the morning let us thank God for the rest of the night in "the name of the Lord Jesus," and in His name let us at night thank Him for the mercies of the day. The ordinary daily life, full of most ordinary duties, will thus be lightened by the thought of what God has done for us for Christ's sake. Each ordinary deed will lead to thankfulness that He has given us the power to perform it. At first it may seem impossible to remember the Lord Jesus in everything and to do all in His name, yet the mere endeavor will strengthen us. Even as a mother is conscious of her love for her little child all through the day's hard work, so the love of Christ will enable us to live all day in His presence. We need to completely surrender ourselves—to live for God all the day.

I have often spoken and written of what it means to pray in the name of Christ. On reading our text of today I thought: Here we have the right explanation. The man who does all in word and deed, in the name of Jesus, may have the full, childlike confidence that what he asks in that name he will receive. Take the text into your heart and you may count on the Holy Spirit to make it true in your life.

The Spirit Glorifies Christ

He will glorify Me, for He will take of what is Mine and declare it to you.

John 16:14

TO understand the work of the Holy Spirit and truly to experience it, one must try to grasp the relationship of the Holy Spirit to the Lord Jesus. Our Lord said definitely, before His departure, that the Spirit would come as a Helper to the disciples. *The Spirit* would reveal Him in their hearts *in heavenly glory*. The disciples were full of the thought. They would not miss their Lord but have Him with them always! This made them pray earnestly for the Holy Spirit, for they longed to have Jesus with them always. This was the promise of the Master: The Spirit would reveal Him to them.

This is the meaning of our text: "The Spirit will glorify Me"—even as I am in the glory of heaven, He will make Me known. "He will take of what is Mine"—My love, My joy, My peace, and all My life—"and declare it to you." Where there is an earnest desire for the glory of Jesus in the heart of the believer, the Holy Spirit will preserve the holy presence of Jesus in our hearts all the day. We must not weary ourselves with striving after God's presence. We must quietly endeavor to abide in fellowship with Christ always, to love Him and keep His commandments, and to do all things, in word and deed, in the name of Jesus. Then shall we be able to count upon the secret but powerful working of the Spirit within us.

We see again the value of remembering and meditating on the text in Galatians 5:22–23. If our thoughts are always occupied with the Lord Jesus, His love, His joy, His peace—then the Holy Spirit will graciously bring these fruits to ripeness within us. The great desire of the Holy Spirit and of the Father is that Christ may be glorified in and through us. Let it be the earnest desire and prayer of our lives too!

Praying in the Holy Spirit

Praying in the Holy Spirit, keep yourselves in the love of God.
Jude 20–21

P AUL began the last section of the epistle to the
Ephesians with the words: "Be strong in the Lord
and in the power of His might" (6:10). He speaks of the
whole armor of God, and closes by saying that this
armor must be put on with prayer and supplication,
"praying always . . . in the Spirit" (6:18). As the Christian needs to be strong in the Lord all the day, and
to wear his armor against the foe the whole day, so
he needs to live always praying in the Spirit.

The Holy Spirit will not come to us, nor work within
us, just at certain times when we think we need His aid.
The Spirit comes to be our life-companion. He wants us
wholly in His possession at all times, otherwise He cannot
do His work in us. Many Christians do not understand
this. They want the Spirit to help and to teach them,
but do not grasp the truth that He must dwell in them
continually and have full possession of all their being.

When once this truth is grasped, we shall realize that
it is possible to live always "praying in the Holy Spirit."
By faith we may have the assurance that the Spirit will
keep us in a prayerful attitude, and make us realize God's
presence, so that our prayer will be the continual exercise
of fellowship with God and His great love. But as long as
we regard the work of the Spirit as restricted to certain

times and seasons, it will remain an unsolved mystery and a possible stone of offense.

The apostle Jude expresses the same thought as St. Paul when he says: "Praying in the Holy Spirit, keep yourselves in the love of God." This is what each child of God desires and what the Spirit will do within him—keeping him in the love of God, even as I may keep in the sunlight all day long. It is this blessed nearness of God which can enable me to abide in His love at all times, even in the busiest moments of my life, praying without ceasing, in entire dependence on Him.

The Temple of God

Do you not know that you are the temple of God and that the Spirit of God dwells in you? . . . The temple of God is holy, which temple you are.

First Corinthians 3:16–17

FROM eternity it was God's desire to create man for a dwelling in which to show forth His glory. Through man's sin this plan was a seeming failure. In His people Israel God sought a means of carrying out His plan. He would have a house in the midst of His people—first a tabernacle, and then a temple—in which He could dwell. This was but a shadow and image of the true indwelling of God in redeemed mankind, who would be His temple to eternity. So we are built up "into a holy temple . . . for a dwelling place of God in the Spirit" (Eph. 2:21–22).

In the meantime, since the Holy Spirit has been poured forth, He has His dwelling in each heart that has been cleansed and renewed by the Spirit. The message comes to each believer, however feeble he may be: "Do you not know?"—"Do you not know that you are the temple of God?" How little this truth is known or experienced. And yet how true it is: "The temple of God is holy, which temple you are."

Paul testifies of himself: "Christ lives in me" (Gal 2:20). This is the fullness of the gospel which he preached: the riches of the glory of the mystery, Christ in you (see

Col. 1:27). This is what he prayed for so earnestly for believers, that God would strengthen them through His Spirit in the inner man, so that Christ might dwell in their hearts by faith. Yes, this is what our Lord Himself promised: "If anyone loves Me, he will keep My word; and My Father will love him, and *We will come* to him and *make Our home* with him" (John 14:23). Is it not strange that Christians are so slow to receive and to adore this wonder of grace?

It is through the Holy Spirit that you will be sanctified into a temple of God, and you will experience that Christ, with the Father, will take up His home in your heart. Do you desire that the Holy Spirit should teach you to pray? He will do it on this one condition, that you surrender yourself wholly to His guidance.

The Fellowship of the Spirit

The communion of the Holy Spirit be with you.
Second Corinthians 13:14

IN this verse we have one of the chief characteristics and activities of the Holy Spirit. It is the Holy Spirit through whom the Father and Son are one, and through whom They have fellowship with each other in the Godhead. For the Holy Spirit is the true life of the Godhead.

We have fellowship with the Father and the Son through the Spirit. "Our fellowship is with the Father and with His Son" (1 John 1:3). "By this we know that He abides in us, by the Spirit whom He has given us" (3:24). Through the Spirit we know and experience the fellowship of love in daily life with the Father and Son.

Through the Spirit we, as God's children, have fellowship one with another. In the child of God there should be nothing of the selfishness and self-interest that seeks its own welfare. We are members of one body. "There is one body and one Spirit" (Eph. 4:4). And through the Spirit the unity of the body must be maintained. One reason that the Spirit does not work with greater power in the church is that the unity of the Spirit is too little sought after. At Pentecost, after ten days spent in united prayer, the one hundred and twenty seemed melted together into one. They received the Spirit in fellowship with one another.

We have sweet fellowship in the bread and wine when we meet at the communion table; we also have fellowship one with another in the trials of other members of the body. Always it is: The fellowship of the Spirit be with you now and evermore. Remember the words of the text in Galatians about the fruits of the Spirit and again present it to the Spirit in prayer, and so make manifest our love for all God's children.

In heaven there is an eternal fellowship of love between Father and Son through the Spirit. Do we really long to be filled with the Spirit? Let us offer ourselves to God, beseeching Him to grant us the unity and the fellowship of the Spirit with all members of Christ's Body.

With the Whole Heart

You will seek Me and find Me, when you search for Me with all your heart.

Jeremiah 29:13

YOU have often heard it said that if one seeks to perform any great work, he must do it *with his whole heart and with all his powers.* In worldly affairs this is the secret of success and of victory. And even more so in divine things it is indispensable, especially in praying for the Holy Spirit.

I cannot too earnestly or too urgently repeat that the Holy Spirit desires to have full possession of you. He can be satisfied with nothing less if He is to show His full power in your life. He has the right. Why? Because He is the almighty God.

Have you ever realized when you pray for the Holy Spirit *that you are praying for the whole Godhead to take possession of you?* Do you really understand this? Or have your prayers had a wrong motive? Were you expecting that God would do something in your heart, but as to the rest of your activities, you must be free to do your own will? That would be a great mistake. The Holy Spirit must have *full* possession.

You say, that is just the trouble. You do not feel such a burning, urgent desire as you ought, and you do not see any chance of its becoming true in your life. God knows about this impotence of yours; He has therefore ordained in His divine providence that the Holy Spirit shall work within you all you need. What God commands and demands of us, *He will Himself work within us.* On our part there must be earnest prayer to the Father each day, and an acceptance of the Holy Spirit as our Leader and Guide.

Child of God, the Holy Spirit longs to possess you wholly. Take time to give Him your answer, and cast yourself in complete dependence and impotence on the word of His promise, and on His almighty power at work within you.

The Love of God in Our Hearts

The love of God has been poured out in our hearts by the Holy Spirit who was given to us.

Romans 5:5

THE Holy Spirit is poured out in our hearts by God the Father. The love of God is poured out in our hearts through the Holy Spirit. As truly as God has poured forth the Spirit, so truly is the love of God shed forth by the Spirit.

Why do we so seldom experience this? Simply because of our unbelief. It takes time to believe in the divine, mighty working of the Holy Spirit through whom our hearts are filled with the love of God. We need time for retirement from the world and its interests for our souls to bask in the light of God so that the eternal love may take possession of our hearts. If we believe in the infinite love of God and the divine power with which He takes possession of the heart, then we will receive what we ask for—the love of God poured out in our hearts by the Holy Spirit. God desires His children to love Him with all their hearts and all their strength. He knows how impotent we are. And for that very reason He has given the Spirit, who searches the deep things of God and in these depths has found the fountain of eternal love, to fill our hearts with His love to His Son.

If you long for this, draw nigh to God and abide there in quiet worship and adoration, and you will know the love of God in Christ which passes all knowledge (see Eph. 3:19).

The Holy Spirit wants to have you wholly. He will teach you each day to dwell as a little child with the Father in His great love, and to abide in the love of Christ each day and to show forth that love towards the brethren and towards a perishing world. He will make your heart a fountain of everlasting love, springing up to life eternal, and flowing forth in blessing to all around. Say with a heart full of thanksgiving: "The love of God is poured out in my heart through the Holy Spirit."

Walk in the Spirit

Walk in the Spirit. . . . If we live in the Spirit, let us also walk in the Spirit.

Galatians 5:16, 25

THE word "walk" reminds us of daily life with our fellow men. The Christian in his walk and conversation must follow the leading of the Spirit and walk *by the Spirit*. That will be the chief sign of the spiritual man, who serves God in the new way of the Spirit and does not trust in the flesh.

People speak as though the Spirit were only needed in our intercourse with God when we pray, or for our work in the service of the kingdom. This is a great mistake. God gives us His Spirit to be in us the whole day. We need Him most in the midst of our daily work, because the world has then such power to lead us away from God. We need to pray to the Father every morning for a fresh portion of His Spirit for each day. During the course of the day let us remind ourselves that the Spirit is with us, and lift up our hearts to God, remembering that Christ thus abides with us always.

Paul says: "As you therefore have received Christ Jesus the Lord, so walk in Him" (Col. 2:6); and again: "Put on the Lord Jesus Christ" (Rom. 13:14). As I put on my cloak when I go out, so the Christian must put on the Lord Jesus, and show by his conduct that Christ lives in him and that he walks by the Spirit.

"Walk in the Spirit, and you shall not fulfill the lust of the flesh" (Gal. 5:16). As long as we are not under the guidance of the Holy Spirit, the flesh will rule over us. Oh, that we knew the unspeakable value of the grace that God has given! The Spirit of His Son in our hearts will cry "Abba, Father," so that we may walk the whole day in God's presence as His beloved children. Christian, learn this lesson: the Spirit is given you to teach you that you may walk by the Spirit at all times. Thank God continually for this divine Leader, who gives us daily renewal from heaven and enables us to walk and to abide in Christ.

The Spirit Promised to the Obedient

If you love Me, keep My commandments. And I will pray the Father, and He will give you another Helper.

John 14:15–16

CHRIST would, before long, ascend to heaven and there pray the Father to send the Helper, the Holy Spirit. He would not only do this once, but it would form part of His intercessory work. He would remain "always liv[ing] to make intercession" (Heb. 7:25). The continual communication of the Spirit of the Father comes through the Son.

The Lord tells us here on what conditions He will send the Spirit. If we love Him and keep His commandments: thereupon "I will pray the Father." This is a word of deep meaning, a searching word—a word of greatly needed and blessed teaching. The Holy Spirit is given to us to enable us to do the will of the Father. The condition is reasonable and just, that as far as we have kept the commandments through the Spirit, the Spirit will be granted to us in fuller measure. As we heartily accept this truth and yield ourselves willingly to the Spirit's guidance, we shall receive from day to day the fullness of the Spirit. Let us say to God that we accept the condition with all our heart and will strive to keep His commands, and then ask for power to do His commandments more perfectly.

Do not listen to the whispers of Satan or give way to unbelief and sloth. Surrender yourself unreservedly to the Lord who has said: "If you love Me, keep My commandments." Love will enable you to do it. The Lord Jesus does not deceive us with a vain hope in this matter. No, He gives the grace, He gives His own love in our hearts, teaching us to say: "I delight to do Your will" (Ps. 40:8). Let us trust Him with childlike faith and give ourselves wholly—that is all that is necessary—to do His will. Then the beauty of the divine agreement that He makes with us will dawn upon us: "If you keep My commandments, you will abide in My love" (John 15:10), and the Father will send the Holy Spirit anew each day.

Spiritual or Carnal?

And I, brethren, could not speak to you as to spiritual people
but as to carnal, as to babes in Christ.

First Corinthians 3:1

THE apostle here uses three words describing the spiritual condition of a man. There is *the natural man*, in his unconverted state—one who cannot "receive the things of the Spirit of God" (1 Cor. 2:14). There is *the spiritual man*, who can discern spiritual things (see 1 Cor. 2:14–15). And between the two there is *the carnal man*, who is called "a babe in Christ" and who lives in jealousy and strife (see 1 Cor. 3:3).

It is important for us to know whether or not we are carnal Christians, giving way to sin and the lusts of the flesh. With the thought that things cannot be otherwise, we are apt to be content to allow much that is sinful and wrong into our lives. God calls us, and the Spirit draws us to be spiritual men and women—that is to say, people who pray each day to be led and guided through the day into a truly spiritual life. When the Lord Jesus promised the Spirit to His disciples, it was in the full expectation that they would yield themselves wholly to the leading and power of the Spirit.

And it is in the same expectation that the Spirit will be granted anew each day, if we yield ourselves unreservedly to be sanctified in all our walk and conversation.

Oh, that our eyes were open to see how right and how blessed this is!

Many Christians pray for the Holy Spirit, but always with a certain reservation, for they intend in many things still to do their own will. O Christian, when you pray, entrust yourself fully to the guidance of the Holy Spirit for the whole day. If there is true willingness on your part, then the Holy spirit will take full possession of you and will preserve and sanctify your life. Do not serve God half-heartedly. Pray for the enlightenment of the Spirit, that you may see the possibility and the blessedness of a life wholly surrendered to His service.

The Spirit of Wisdom

*That . . . the Father . . . may give to you the spirit of wisdom
and revelation in the knowledge of Him, the eyes of your
understanding being enlightened.*

Ephesians 1:17–18

IN the Word of God we find a wonderful combina-
tion of the human and the divine. The language is
that of a man. Anyone who has a good understanding
can grasp the meaning of the words and the truths
contained in them. Yet this is all that man, in the
power of his human understanding, can do.

There is a divine side in which the holy God expresses
His deepest thoughts to us. The carnal man cannot at-
tain to them or comprehend them, for they must be
"spiritually discerned" (1 Cor. 2:14). Only through the
Holy Spirit can the Christian appropriate the divine
truth contained in God's Word. Paul prays earnestly
that God would grant the spirit of wisdom to his readers, eyes that are enlightened through the Holy Spirit
to understand what is written, that they may know the
exceeding greatness of His power working in all who
believe (see Eph. 1:19).

Much of our religion is ineffectual because people
accept the truths of God's Word with the intellect and
strive to put them into practice in their own strength,
but it is only the Holy Spirit who can really reveal divine
truth to us. A young student in a theological seminary

may accept the truths of God's Word as head knowledge even while the Word has little power in his heart, failing to lead him to a life of joy and peace in the Lord Jesus. Paul teaches us that when we read God's Word or meditate on it, we should pray: "Father, grant me the spirit of wisdom and revelation" (see Eph. 1:17). As we do this each day, we shall find that God's Word is living and powerful and will work experientially in our hearts. God's commands will be changed into promises. His commands are for our good and not grievous, and the Holy Spirit will teach us to do lovingly and joyfully all that He has commanded.

The Spirit of Sanctification

Elect . . . in sanctification of the Spirit, for obedience and sprinkling of the blood of Jesus Christ.

First Peter 1:2

IN the Old Testament God was revealed as the thrice-holy One. The Spirit is mentioned more than a hundred times, but only three times as the Holy Spirit. But in the New Testament the word "holy" is ascribed frequently to the Spirit, and we are told that Christ sanctified Himself for us that we might be holy. The great work of the Holy Spirit is to glorify Christ in us as *our sanctification.*

Has this truth ever taken hold of you—at church prayer meetings or in your private devotions—that the great object for which the Holy Spirit is given is to *sanctify* you? If you do not accept this truth, then the Holy Spirit cannot do His purifying work. If you only want the Spirit to help you to be a little better and to pray a little more, you will not get very far. But when you once understand that He has the name "Holy Spirit" because His distinct ministry is to impart God's holiness and that He desires to sanctify you wholly, then you will begin to realize why the Holy Spirit dwells in your heart.

And what will be the result? You will feel that He must have you *wholly.* He must rule and control the whole day. My life and conversation must be in the *Spirit.* My prayer, my faith, my fellowship with the Father, and all my work in God's service, must be completely under His sway. For, as the Spirit of holiness, He is the Spirit of my sanctification.

Dear brothers and sisters, what I have just said is deep, eternal truth. Even if we are willing to accept this truth, and meditate on it daily, it will be of no avail if we do not wait upon God to grant us the Spirit of heavenly wisdom and a vision of what God has intended for us in His wonderful gift, the Spirit of sanctification. Each morning, receive the gift. Say slowly and calmly: "Abba, Father, for this new day, renew within me the gift of Your Holy Spirit."

Rivers of Living Water

He who believes in Me . . . out of his heart will flow rivers of living water.

John 7:38

OUR Lord, in His conversation with the Samaritan woman, said: "The water that I shall give him will become in him a fountain of water springing up into everlasting life" (John 4:14). In our text the promise is even greater: rivers of living waters flowing from the believer, bringing life and blessing to *others*. John says further that this refers to the Holy Spirit, who was to come when Christ had been glorified, for the Holy Spirit was not yet poured out. The Spirit of God was mentioned in the Old Testament, but the Holy Spirit had not yet been given. Christ must first be offered through the eternal Spirit (on the cross) (see Heb. 9:14), be raised from the dead by the Spirit of holiness (see Rom. 1:4), and receive authority from the Father to send forth the Holy Spirit. Then only would the Christian be able to say: Now the Holy Spirit of Christ is in me.

What do we need in order to experience these two wonderful promises— the well of water and the rivers of living water? Just one thing—inner attachment to Christ, with unreserved surrender to Him for daily fellowship. This leads to firm assurance that His Spirit will work in us what we cannot do. This is all summed up in the words

He who believes in Me. It is a *continuing* belief. We need a faith that rejoices in Christ's divine might and love, and depends on Him day by day to grant us grace so that living water may flow forth from us.

If the water from a reservoir is to flow into a house all day, one thing is necessary—the connection must be perfect; then the water passes through the pipe of its own accord. So the union between you and Christ must be uninterrupted. Your faith must accept Christ and depend on Him to sustain the new life.

Let your faith rejoice that Jesus Christ gives us the Holy Spirit. May you have assurance that the Holy Spirit is within you as a fountain of blessing.

Joy in God

The kingdom of God is . . . righteousness and peace and joy in the Holy Spirit.

Romans 14:17

Now may the God of hope fill you with all joy and peace in believing . . . by the power of the Holy Spirit.

15:13

A Christian man said to me, shortly after his conversion: "I always thought that if I became religious it would be impossible for me to do my worldly business. The two things seemed so contrary. I seemed to be a man trying to dig a vineyard with a bag of sand on his shoulders. But when I found the Lord, I was so filled with joy that I could do my work cheerfully from morning till night. The bag of sand was gone; the joy of the Lord was my strength for all my work."

Truly a significant lesson. Many Christians do not understand that the joy of the Lord will keep them and fit them for their daily work. Even slaves, when filled with the love of Christ, have been able to testify to the happiness that He gives.

Read the two texts at the heading of this chapter and note how the kingdom of God is pure joy and peace through the Holy Spirit and how God will, if we believe, "fill [us] with all joy and peace . . . by the power of the Holy Spirit." Then try to grasp the fact that the

Holy Spirit will produce this joy and peace of Christ in *our* hearts—yes, *ours*! To many Christians the thought of submission to the Holy Spirit is a matter of grief and self-reproach, of desire and disappointment—something too high and holy for them. What a foolish situation, that the great gift of the Father, meant to keep us in the joy and peace of Christ, should become a matter of self-reproach and care!

Remember Galatians 5:22, and listen attentively to the voice of the Spirit each day as He points to Jesus Christ, who offers you this wonderful fruit: "My love, My joy, My peace." "Though now you do not see Him, yet believing, you rejoice with joy inexpressible and full of glory" (1 Pet. 1:8). Pray in all humility to the Holy Spirit, believing firmly that He will lead you into the joy of the Lord.

All the Day—Every Day

Every day I will bless You.

Psalm 145:2

IT is a step forward in the Christian life when one definitely decides to seek to have fellowship with God in His Word each day without fail. His perseverance will be crowned with success if he is really in earnest. His experience may be somewhat as follows:

When he awakes in the morning, God will be his first thought. He will also have a designated time set aside for prayer and will resolve to give God adequate time to hear his requests and to reveal Himself to him. Then he may speak out all his desires to God and expect an answer.

Later on in the day, even if only for a few minutes, he will take time to keep up the fellowship with God. And again in the evening, a quiet period is necessary to review the day's work, and with confession of sin receive the assurance of forgiveness and dedicate himself afresh to God and His service.

Such a one will gradually get an insight into what is lacking in his life, and will be ready to say: Not only "every day" but "all the day." He will realize that the Holy Spirit is in him unceasingly, just as his breathing is continuous. In the inner chamber he will make it his aim to gain the assurance through faith that the Holy Spirit, and the Lord Jesus, and the Father Himself will grant Their presence and help all through the day.

All the day! Christian, the Holy Spirit says: "Today." "Behold, now is the accepted time" (2 Cor. 6:2)!

A man who had undergone a serious operation asked his doctor, "How long will I have to lie here?" And the answer came: "Only a day at a time." And that is the law of the Christian life. God gave the manna daily; there was a morning and evening sacrifice on the altar. By these God showed that His children should live by the day. Seek this day to trust to the leading of the Holy Spirit the *whole day*. You need not care for the morrow, but rest in the assurance that He who has led you today will draw still nearer tomorrow.

The Spirit and the Cross

*The blood of Christ, who through the eternal Spirit offered
Himself without spot to God, [shall] cleanse your conscience
from dead works to serve the living God.*

Hebrews 9:14

THE connection between the cross and the Spirit
is inconceivably close and full of meaning. The
Spirit brought Christ to the cross and enabled Him
to die there. The cross was to Christ and to the Spirit
the culmination point of Their desire on earth. The
cross gave Christ the right to pray down the Holy
Spirit on earth, because He had there made reconcili-
ation for sin. The cross gave Christ the right and the
power to grant us the power of the Spirit, because
on it He freed us from the power of sin.

To put it briefly: Christ could not have attained to
the heavenly life, or have poured out the Holy Spirit, if
He had not first died to sin, to the world, and to His own
life. He died to sin that He might live to God. And that is
the way the Holy Spirit brings the cross into our hearts. It
is only as those who have been *crucified* with Christ that
we can receive the full power of the Spirit. It is because
we do not realize how necessary it is to die to all earthly
things, that the Spirit cannot gain full possession of us.

How is it so few Christians understand or experience that the fellowship of the Spirit is a fellowship of
the cross? Simply because they do not feel the need of

praying for the Spirit of wisdom to give them a deep, spiritual insight into the oneness of the Spirit and the cross. They try to use their human understanding, but there is too little waiting upon God to teach them divine truths through the Spirit.

Brothers and sisters, begin today to ask God to grant you a sight of how the Spirit will take you to the cross of Christ, in fellowship with Him, to die to the world and to sin so that all things may become new, and you will actually live and walk and work and pray in the Spirit to the glory of God.

The Spirit and the Blood

*There are three that bear witness . . . the Spirit, the water,
and the blood; and these three agree as one.*

First John 5:8

THE water is external, a sign of the renewing and
purifying through regeneration used in baptism.
The Spirit and the blood are two spiritual expres-
sions, working together in regeneration: the blood
for the forgiveness of sins, the Spirit for the renewal
of the whole nature. All through life the Spirit and
the blood must agree.

The oneness is spiritual and true. Through the
blood we obtain the Spirit, as through the blood we are
redeemed and purified unto it to receive the Spirit. Only
through the blood can we with confidence pray for and
receive the Spirit. O Christian, if you would have boldness each day to trust to the guidance of the Spirit, then
let your faith in the precious blood be sure and strong.

There may be some sin in your life of which you are
hardly conscious, but which grieves the Spirit and drives
Him away. The only way to avoid this is to believe that
"The blood of Jesus Christ . . . cleanses [you] from all
sin" (1:7). Your only right to approach God is through
the blood of the Lamb. Come with every sin, known or
unknown, and plead the blood of Christ as your only
claim on the love that accepts and forgives.

Nevertheless, do not rest content with the forgiveness of sins, but accept the fullness of the Spirit, to which the blood gives you access. In the Old Testament the priest went into the Holy Place with the blood, and the high priest into the Holiest of All. With the blood Christ entered the heavenly sanctuary and from there poured out the Holy Spirit. Do not for a moment doubt that you have a right through the blood to the fullness of the Spirit.

As one who has been redeemed by the blood of Christ, make a complete surrender of yourself to God as His purchased possession, a vessel ready for Him to use, a dwelling-place of the Holy Spirit.

The Spirit in Preacher and Hearer

Our gospel [came to you] . . . in power, and in the Holy Spirit and in much assurance. . . . And you became followers of us . . . having received the word . . . with joy of the Holy Spirit.

First Thessalonians 1:5–6
(See also First Corinthians 2:4–5)

PAUL more than once reminds his converts that the chief characteristic of his preaching was t*he power—the supernatural power of the Holy Spirit.* The Holy Spirit was so imparted to his hearers that they received the word "with joy of the Holy Spirit."

This is one of the most important lessons in the spiritual life. We, as hearers, are so accustomed to listen attentively to the sermon to see what it has to teach us that we are apt to forget that the blessing of our church-going depends on two things. First, the prayer for the preacher, that he may speak "in demonstration of the Spirit and of power" (1 Cor. 2:4); and then, the prayer for the congregation and for ourselves, that we may receive the word, not from man, but as it is in truth, God's Word, "which . . . effectively works in you who believe" (1 Thess. 2:13). Alas, how often there is no manifestation of the Spirit—when both the speaking and the hearing are mainly the work of human understanding or feeling. So often there is no power that raises the soul with spiritual insight into the life of faith that God has provided for His children.

How earnestly we should pray that God may reveal to us all, both minister and people, "*the spirit of wisdom and revelation*" (Eph. 1:17), that we may discover what the place really is that the Holy Spirit should have in our lives, and what the perfect work is that He will do within us! God help us to learn this dual prayer! Then we shall understand what Christ meant when He said: "*Go not, preach not*—but *wait* for the Promise of the Father," and "you shall be witnesses to Me . . . to the end of the earth" (see Acts 1:4–8).

Pray earnestly that God may teach us to pray down the power of the Holy Spirit upon ministers and missionaries and their congregations, that the preaching may be in the manifestation of the Spirit and of power, for the conversion and sanctification of souls.

The Full Gospel

Then Peter said: Repent . . . for the remission of sins; and you shall receive the gift of the Holy Spirit.

Acts 2:38

WHEN John the Baptist preached "Repent, for the kingdom of heaven is at hand" (Matt. 3:2), he also said: "He who is coming after me . . . will baptize you with the Holy Spirit and fire" (3:11). When Christ preached the gospel of the kingdom He said: "There are some standing here who shall not taste death till they see the Son of Man coming in His kingdom" (16:28). This is what happened at the outpouring of the Holy Spirit. Peter preached, on that day of Pentecost, the full gospel of repentance and forgiveness of sins, *and the gift of the Holy Spirit*. This is indispensable in preaching the gospel, for then only is it possible for a Christian to live in the will of God and to please Him in all things. The kingdom of God is righteousness (in Christ), and joy (in God) through the Holy Spirit. The continuous joy of which Christ speaks, "My joy" (John 15:11), can only be obtained through the power of the Holy Spirit.

How often only half the gospel is preached—conversion and forgiveness of sins—and souls are led no further into the truth. The knowledge and appropriation of the life of the Spirit within us is not mentioned. No wonder that so many Christians fail to understand that they must depend each day on the Spirit for the joy which will be their strength.

Dear Christian, accept this truth for yourself, as well as for those among whom you labor—that the daily enjoyment of the leading of God's Spirit is indispensable for a joyous life of faith. If you feel that there has been a lack in your spiritual life, then begin at once to pray the Father to grant you the gift of the Holy Spirit anew each day. Then trust yourself to His leading and guidance all the day. Let the remembrance of the text in Galatians 5:22–23 give you courage for all that the Holy Spirit will do for you. Regard your heart constantly as a garden of the Lord in which the Holy Spirit will bear abundant fruit to the glory of God.

The Ministry of the Spirit

You are an epistle of Christ, ministered by us, written . . . by the Spirit of the living God . . . on tablets of flesh, that is, of the heart.

Second Corinthians 3:3

THE Corinthians' church was a "letter of recommendation" for Paul, showing how much he had done for them. Although he claimed nothing for himself, God had enabled him as a "minister of the Spirit" to write in their hearts "with the Spirit of the living God." He himself declared: "Not that we are sufficient of ourselves to think of anything as being from ourselves, but our sufficiency is from God, who also made us sufficient as ministers of the new covenant" (3:5–6).

What a wonderful presentation of the work of a minister for his people! A preacher prepared to be a minister of the Spirit, with power to write in the hearts of his people the name and the love of Christ. No wonder that when speaking of the glory that was upon the face of Moses when he communed with God (see 3:7–11), Paul says, "the ministry of righteousness exceeds much more in glory . . . because of the glory that excels" (3:9–10). He then speaks of how "we all, with unveiled face, beholding as in a mirror the glory of the Lord, are being transformed into the same image from glory to glory, just as by the Spirit of the Lord" (3:18).

Oh that God would restore the ministry of the gospel to its original power! Oh that all ministers and church members would unite in the prayer that God, by the mighty working of His Spirit, would give the ministry of the Spirit its right place, and teach the people to believe that when Christ is preached to them they are beholding as in a mirror the glory of the Lord, and may be changed into the same image by the Spirit of the Lord!

What a call that is for us to persevere in the prayer that the Holy Spirit may again have His rightful place in the ministry of the Word, so that the exceeding and abundant glory of this ministry may be manifested.

The Spirit from Heaven

It was . . . reported to you through those who have preached the gospel to you by the Holy Spirit sent from heaven.

First Peter 1:12

CHRIST has taught us to think of God as our own Father in heaven, who is ready to bestow His blessings on His children on earth. Our Lord Himself was taken up into the glory of heaven, and we are told that we are seated with Him in the heavenly places, being in Christ. Then the Holy Spirit comes to us from heaven to pour into our hearts all the light, and the love, and the joy, and the power of heaven.

Those who are truly filled with the Spirit have a heavenly life in themselves. Their walk and conversation are in heaven. They are in daily fellowship with the Father and with the Son. They seek the things that are above, for their life is hid with Christ in God (see Col. 3:3). Their chief characteristic is heavenly-mindedness. They carry about with them the marks of their eternal, heavenly destiny.

How can one cultivate this heavenly disposition? By allowing the Holy Spirit, sent from heaven, to do His heavenly work in our hearts and to bring to ripeness in our souls the fruits of the Spirit which grow in the paradise of God. The Spirit will raise our hearts daily to fellowship with God in heaven and will teach us to dwell in the heavenlies with Him. The Spirit not only makes the glorified Christ in heaven present in our hearts but He teaches us to dwell in His abiding presence. O Christian, take time each day to receive from the Father the continual guidance of the Holy Spirit. Let Him overcome the world for you and strengthen you as a child of heaven to walk daily with your God and with the Lord Jesus. Do not be unbelieving. The Holy Spirit will do His part if you in faith surrender yourself to His control. You will learn to speak to others with such heavenly joy that you will draw them, too, to give themselves to the leading of the Spirit and to walk in the heavenly joy of Christ's love.

The Spirit and Prayer

*Most assuredly, I say to you, whatever you ask the Father in
My name He will give you.*

John 16:23

IN our Lord's Farewell Discourse (see John 13–17), He
presented the life in the dispensation of the Spirit in
all its power and attractiveness. One of the most glori-
ous results of the day when the Holy Spirit should come
would be the *new power* that man would have to pray
down from heaven the power of God to bless the world.
Seven times we have the promise repeated: "Whatever
you ask in My name, that I will do" (see John 14:13, 14;
15:7, 16; 16:23, 24, 26). Read these passages over, that
you may come to understand fully how urgently and
earnestly our Lord repeated the promise.

In the power of the perfect salvation that Christ ac-
complished, in the power of His glory with the Father,
in the power of the outpouring of the third Person of the
Godhead—the Holy Spirit—to dwell in the hearts of His
servants, they would have the unspeakable freedom to
ask what they desired of the fullness of the will of God,
and it should be done. Everything was included in these
few words: "*Whatever you ask in My name, that I will do.*"

During the ten days before Pentecost the disciples
put this to the proof. Then, in response to their continuous united prayer the heavens were opened and the Spirit
of God descended to earth to dwell in their hearts, filling

them with His life-power. They received this life-giving power of the Spirit that they might impart it to thousands more. That power is *still* the pledge for all time of *what God will do*. If God's children will agree with one accord to wait for the promise of the Father each day, there is no limit to what God will do for them!

O Christian, remember that you are living in the dispensation of the Spirit. That means that the Holy Spirit will dwell in you with heavenly power, enabling you to testify for Him. But it also means that you may unite with God's children to ask in prayer greater and more wonderful things than the heart has even conceived.

With One Accord in Prayer

These all continued with one accord in prayer..

Acts 1:14

When the Day of Pentecost had fully come . . . they were all filled with the Holy Spirit.

2:1–4

OUR Lord gave the command to His disciples: "Go into all the world and preach the gospel to every creature" (Mark 16:15), and He added the promise: "Lo, I am with you always" (Matt. 28:20). We may be fully assured that this command and this promise were not meant alone for the disciples, *but also for us, their followers.*

Just before His ascension Christ gave His very last command, also with a promise attached to it. The command was: Go not, preach not—"wait for the Promise of the Father" (Acts 1:4). And the promise was: "You shall receive power when the Holy Spirit has come upon you; and you shall be witnesses to Me . . . to the end of the earth" (1:8). *This very last command and promise are also meant for us.* As irrevocable as the command "*Preach* the gospel" (Mark 16:15), with its accompanying promise, is this last command of all, to *wait* for the promise of the Father—and "you shall receive [the] power [of] the Holy Spirit."

For ten days the disciples pled that promise with one accord, and their prayer was wonderfully answered. Alas, that the church of our day has tried to carry out the first command, "Preach the gospel," but has too often forgotten the second, "Wait for the promise of the Father." The call comes to each believer to *pray daily with one accord* for this great gift of the Holy Spirit. Many Christians who pray for themselves and their own work forget to pray for the church of Christ worldwide. The power of the first disciples lay in the fact that they *as one body* were prepared to forget themselves and to pray for the Holy Spirit over all mankind.

O Christian, whatever you may have learned from reading this little book, learn one more lesson. *Daily prayer in fellowship with God's children is indispensable*, and it is a sacred duty if the Spirit is again to come in power. Let not your knowledge of the working of God's Holy Spirit be limited to yourself alone, nor even to your church, but in the world-embracing love of Christ, for the profit of all God's children and His kingdom over the whole world, *pray for power*.

PUBLICATIONS

Fort Washington, PA 19034

This book is published by CLC Publications, an outreach of CLC
Ministries International. The purpose of CLC is to make evangelical
Christian literature available to all nations so that people may come
to faith and maturity in the Lord Jesus Christ. We hope this book has
been life changing and has enriched your walk with God through the
work of the Holy Spirit. If you would like to know more about CLC,
we invite you to visit our website:

www.clcusa.org

To know more about the remarkable story of the founding of
CLC International we encourage you to read

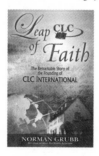

LEAP OF FAITH

Norman Grubb

Paperback
Size 5¹/₄ x 8, Pages 248
ISBN: 978-0-87508-650-7
ISBN (e-book): 978-1-61958-055-8

THE SECRET OF THE FAITH LIFE

Andrew Murray

How can a feeble faith in an almighty Christ move mountains? Part of Andrew Murray's classic *Secret Series* devotionals, *The Secret of the Faith Life* provides insight into the need, power, and blessedness of a wholehearted faith in Jesus and an unreserved surrender to Him, so that we can be prepared to receive Him in the fullness of His love and abiding presence.

Paperback
Size 4¹/₄ x 7, Pages 69
ISBN: 978-1-61958-270-5
ISBN (*e-book*): 978-1-61958-271-2

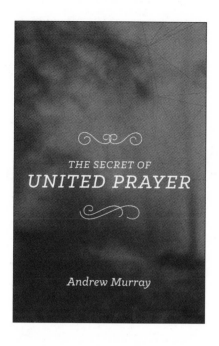

THE SECRET OF UNITED PRAYER

Andrew Murray

Part of the classic *Secret Series*, *The Secret of United Prayer* contains one month of daily selections on the power of united prayer. Murray expresses his desire that many would join the ranks of intercessors—those who pray continually, in unison, for the church of Christ and His kingdom on earth. He studies the "lost" secret of Pentecost: the sure promise that the power of the Holy Spirit will be given in answer to fervent prayer.

Paperback
Size 4¹/₄ x 7, Pages 67
ISBN: 978-1-61958-272-9
ISBN (*e-book*): 978-1-61958-273-6

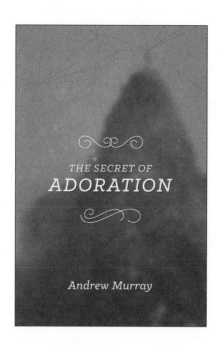

THE SECRET OF ADORATION

Andrew Murray

The Secret Series books contain a wealth of teaching that is based on Andrew Murray's mature and full experience in Christ. *The Secret of Adoration* contains one month of daily selections that highlight the importance of true worship in the lives of believers.

Paperback
Size 4^1/4 x 7, Pages 71
ISBN: 978-1-61958-253-8
ISBN (*e-book*): 978-1-61958-254-5

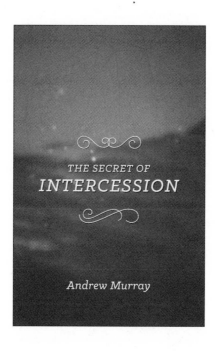

THE SECRET OF INTERCESSION

Andrew Murray

The Secret Series books contain a wealth of teaching that is based on Andrew Murray's mature and full experience in Christ. *The Secret of Intercession* contains one month of daily selections that reveal the power of intercession.

Paperback
Size 4¹/₄ x 7, Pages 67
ISBN: 978-1-61958-249-1
ISBN (*e-book*): 978-1-61958-250-7